Sky Mountain & the Toad

Sky Mountain and the Toad

A fairytale of psychedelic healing and integration through embodiment.

Written by Linda Barnard
Illustrated by Evelyn Shane

Copyright 2026 Linda Barnard
All Rights Reserved.
Published by Sky Mountain Press,
Katy, Texas
ISBN 979-8-218-88623-3

The purpose of the fairytale is threefold: To shed awareness and advocate for the immense healing power of psychedelic assisted psychotherapy, as psychoeducation and integration for clients interested in psychedelic healing, and it is an attempt to translate the ineffable.

Linda Barnard is a psychotherapist in Houston, Texas in private practice. She facilitates ketamine- assisted therapeutic retreats and individual ketamine- assisted psychotherapy. She is passionate about this healing modality and wants to share it with the world.

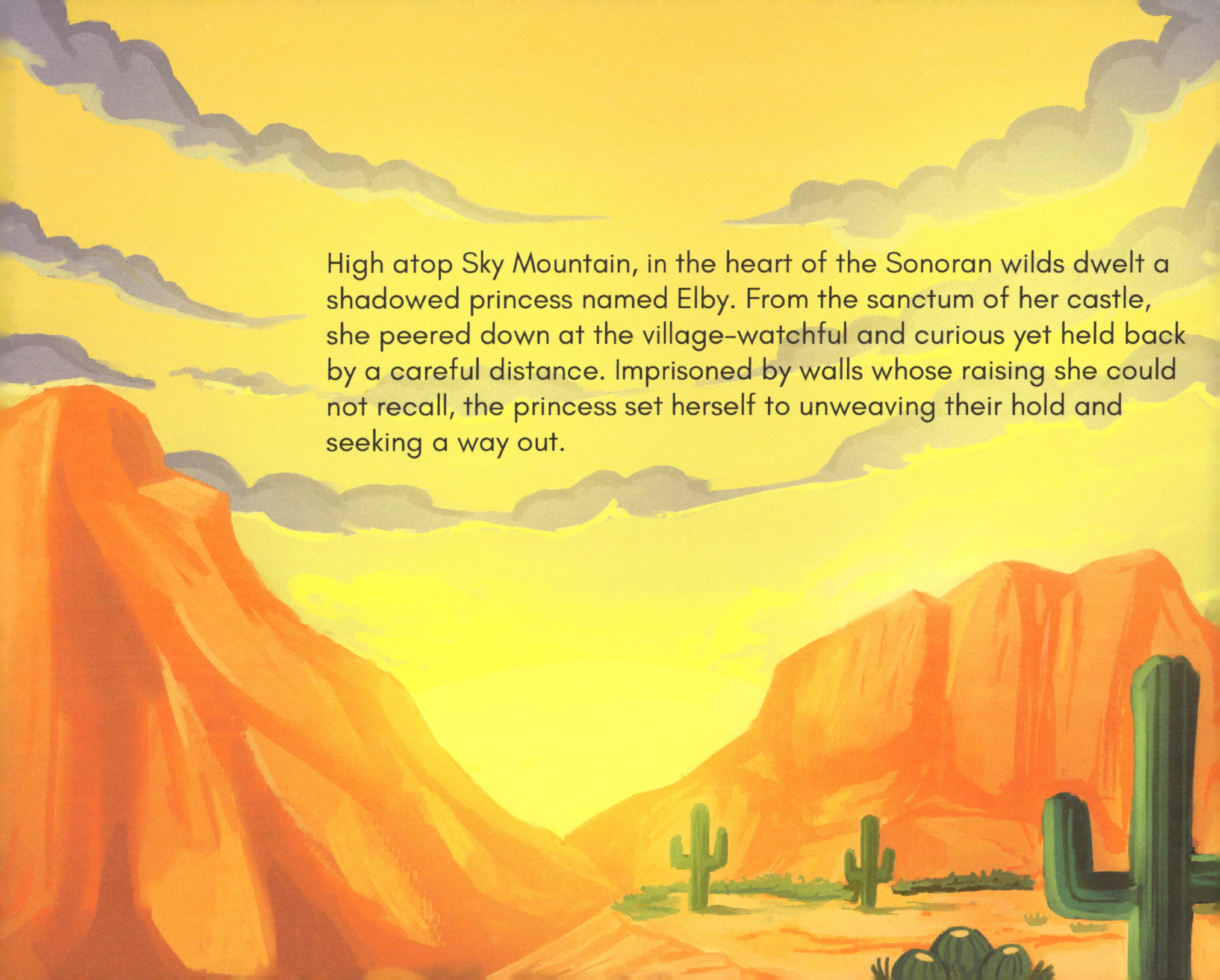

High atop Sky Mountain, in the heart of the Sonoran wilds dwelt a shadowed princess named Elby. From the sanctum of her castle, she peered down at the village-watchful and curious yet held back by a careful distance. Imprisoned by walls whose raising she could not recall, the princess set herself to unweaving their hold and seeking a way out.

She searched to fill the hollowness with books and clothes and trinkets. Yet the princess only heard the ceaseless whirl of thoughts within her head, a private storm that never stilled. Princess Elby wandered trance-like as days became weeks, and months and years, forever in search of a balm to mend the hollow.

One day Princess Elby strolled a familiar path and chanced upon a peculiar toad. "Do you have a name?", asked the princess curiously. The toad replied: "BUFO, but my friends call me Five. Why the long face?" asked Five. "I am bound within these walls, and every trail has led me farther from the freedom I seek".

Five hopped up to gaze into the princess' eyes, winked and whispered "I've been endowed with a powerful elixir that illuminates the pathless path", "Pathless path?" inquired the princess. "You see, explained Five the path you seek has not been traversed. The elixir takes you into unknown territory and you must go alone." Nervously pacing, Princess Elby became unsure that she could manage a journey of such magnitude alone. "Isn't there another way?" she asked.

Five piped in "There are two guides who live just past that saguaro cactus named Baba and Majka. There is a gate armed by two lions, and only those who have strength and bravery are allowed to pass. If you endure their roars the gate will open. Princess Elby knew what she must do and as she approached, the lions let out a deafening roar. The Princess smiled and said "Is that all you've got?" and began pointing a laser away from the gate.

Baba and Majka helped Princess Elby prepare for her journey and then with trepidation and courage she took in the elixir. Within mere seconds a force unknown to the princess sucked her into an energetic vortex. In an instant Princess Elby disappeared and what was left was the infinite, wild energy of the universe coursing through space and time. The castle trembled. Mortar cracked. Walls loosened like pages of a book blown by a sudden gust of wind.

When the dust settled, she could not find the castle or herself. She reached to feel her hands, am I alive? Her breath was a stranger. The disorientation was unsettling, as she tried desperately to find herself. As things came into focus, Baba's warm steady gaze held her own. "Welcome Back". He kneeled close "would you like to feel your toes?" he asked gentle as a lullaby.

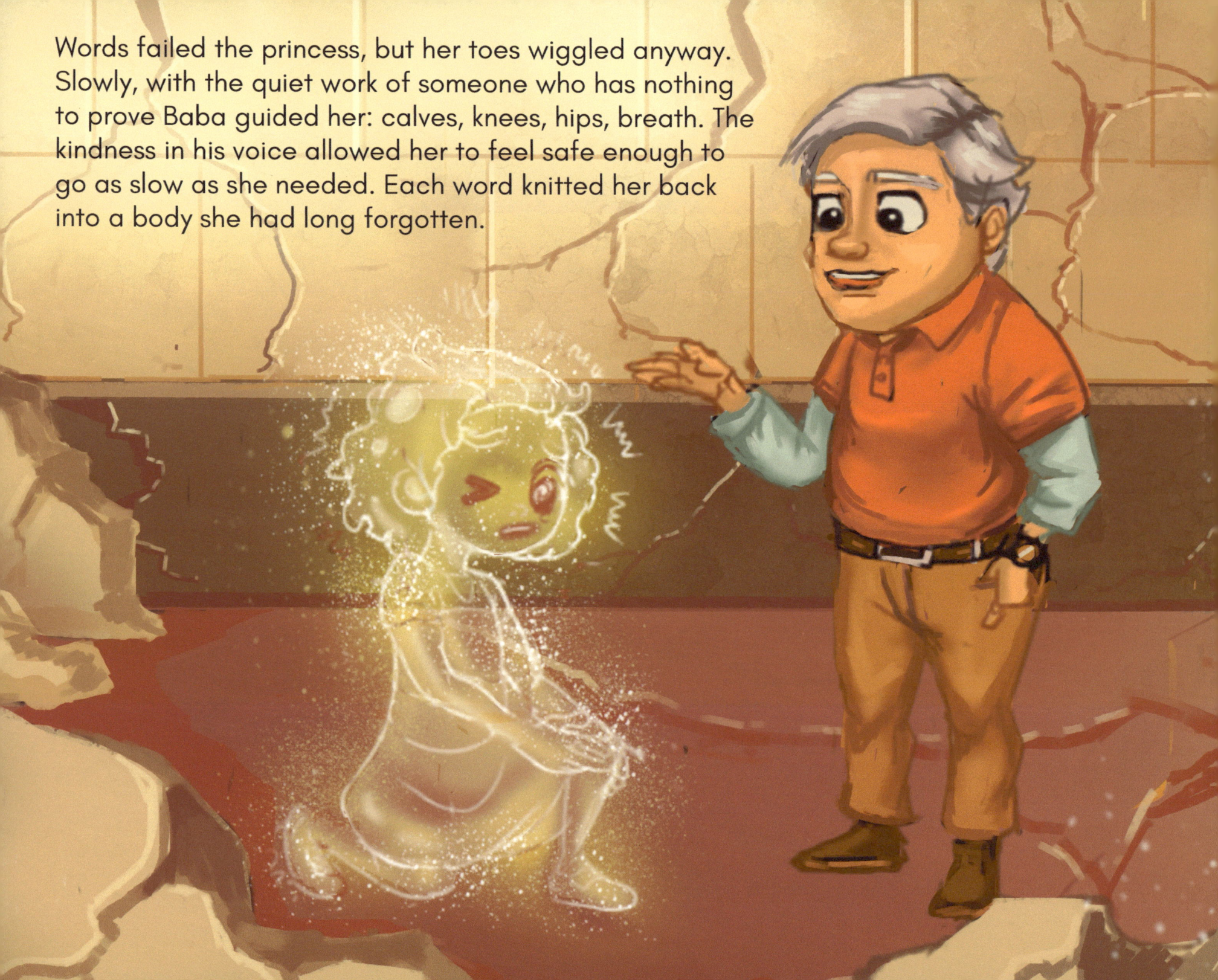

Words failed the princess, but her toes wiggled anyway. Slowly, with the quiet work of someone who has nothing to prove Baba guided her: calves, knees, hips, breath. The kindness in his voice allowed her to feel safe enough to go as slow as she needed. Each word knitted her back into a body she had long forgotten.

The hollowness inside was slowly imbued with aliveness, a divine effervescent light tingling through her spine. Suddenly, the princess realized she was very small and lived inside the warmth of a wiser, older body.
She had no idea!

As she looked up, she saw the same warmth in the eyes of this wise woman, that Baba had so freely given.

The wise woman had tears as she scooped up the princess and pulled her close. "I didn't know you were trapped, and promise to never leave." The princess realized she had been

living within a smaller life looking through dull eyes and muted ears that were stuck in the past.

The next morning, as if she had awakened from a dream, she looked through new set of eyes that were closer to a newborn's than her own. Her ears had opened as wide as the sky. Her skin felt the glorious wind as if it were silk, and sun filled the space that was once hollow.

"I'm alive!" the princess squealed. When she looked in a pool, she saw a whole person looking back- messy, brave and real.

Five sat on a stone and blinked. "You did the work, and you found the path." The woman smiled, "Yes, it was an inside job- I forged the pathless path from up here, to in here."

And so, the love affair began with life, with other people, and with the strange tender body she had at last learned to know.

"FIVE ALIVE!" croaked the toad.

Epilogue

Sky Mountain and the Toad chronicles my debut journey with 5-MEO-DMT, a herculean psychedelic. Language is meaningless and dissolves as the molecule takes hold, the structures of the individual ego-self disintegrate, and a field of experience that is beyond the mind's capacity reveals itself. What transpires here can't be captured entirely through a scientific or medical lens; it is a mystery. Many have tried to put language to the ineffable, who are more skilled in the art of words than myself. The allegory of Sky Mountain and the Toad is my brain's feeble attempt at articulating the ineffable.

What several months of integration revealed
Through group process, meditation, journaling, and quiet walks in nature, I came to know a wounded part of my psyche and began an intimate healing relationship. Spiritual reparenting went from a concept to a reality. It took a few weeks for me to understand and articulate this new paradigm shift in my psyche. An inherently wise, and compassionate state of being seemed to take center stage in my mind. There was a clear separation between ego and what I call "Blue Sky Mind". Initially, I felt a sense of pride around this ability as I claimed it as my own. On a walk as I was feeling prideful and giddy that I had "transcended my ego", I realized that spacious awareness did not belong to me exclusively. I had access to an awareness that was more than my self-constructs. I struggled to understand how this new awareness seemed to suddenly be available, without effort on my part. Webster dictionary defines transpersonal as extending or going beyond the personal or individual. The core idea is that something exists or occurs beyond the confines of the individual self, ego, or personality. That concept tracks onto my experience. I became embodied, meaning to say I had a felt sense of this kind awareness that now informed me who I was beyond the conditioning and self-limiting beliefs. This embodied spacious awareness provides a container for my individual self. As time goes on, the separation between ego and Blue-Sky Mind becomes narrower. The ego- doing what it does- trying to reestablish dominance insidiously. No harm, no foul. Afterall what's a house without a foundation?

The palace as ego and strategy:

The role of the ego is to build our map of reality and imprint the emotional learnings from our childhood. The ego tells us who we are and what the world is. The wizardry is that it all happens outside of conscious awareness, so that it confines us to our convictions of who we are. It serves the purpose of establishing a solid sense of self, and to that means plays an important role in grounding us in our human experience. We unwittingly place ourselves in this self-constructed cage and throw away the key. Psychedelics transcend this egoic conditioning showing us we hold the key to our own freedom. There is a transfer of power where the ego is now held in a bigger container of compassionate awareness.

The palace also represents the walls of dissociation erected as a key strategy growing up in an alcoholic, chaotic, dysfunctional family of origin. This happened in my formative years before language or a sense of self was fully formed. My brain and body learned to abandon parts of myself that were not attuned to or disallowed relationally. Psychedelics can give us access to these dissociated parts that are behind well protected walls. I embodied my young, wounded child who could only be felt because she did not have words. I saw her through imagery, and she communicated through tears, and we connected through attuned attention. I am different post journey. I have a closer relationship with myself as a result.

www.ingramcontent.com/pod-product-compliance
Lightning Source LLC
Chambersburg PA
CBHW042135060526

44119CB00117B/362